Introduction

D0128510

The Nine-Patch is one of the easiest and best-loved quilt blocks ever made. It is popular with beginners because they can easily see how the individual squares and complete quilts are assembled. More experienced quilters use the Nine-Patch to show off interesting color palettes and complex borders. Traditionally, Nine-Patch designs have been limited to geometric compositions, but by slightly altering the nine basic building blocks, it is possible to make recognizable images such as flowers, birds, sailboats and several others as shown in the seven quilts and two pillows in this book. Make any of the quilts for children or use them as wall hangings. Follow the basic pillow instructions and substitute any block to make pillows that fit with your decor.

page **4**

page **14**

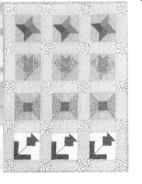

page **26**

General Instructions

The Nine-Patch

The individual squares that make up a Nine-Patch consist of a plain square, halved square (crosswise), halved square (diagonal), quartered square (small squares), quartered square (small triangles) and square with one or more trimmed corners, **Fig 1**.

Fig 1

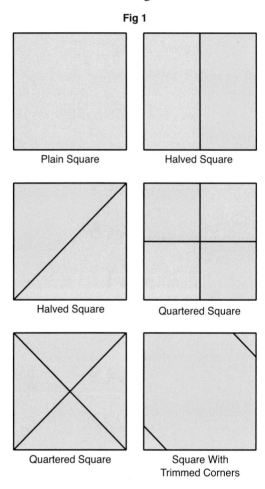

Plain Square   Halved Square

Halved Square   Quartered Square

Quartered Square   Square With Trimmed Corners

When choosing fabric, select 100 percent cottons that are soft to the touch. Solid colors or small-scale patterns work best since the surface area of a pieced Nine-Patch square is 2" or smaller. For shaded images, choose fabrics that are close in hue and value. To suggest depth for backgrounds or drama for focal points, choose fabrics that contrast in hue and value. Before cutting, experiment with a variety of color and pattern combinations.

All seam allowances are ¼". When piecing, press sections often for ease in handling and more accurate assembly. Also, trim threads often.

Pinning & Basting

To secure the quilt top, batting and quilt back, pin with straight dressmaker pins or small safety pins. Be careful when stitching over straight pins. Feed pins slowly under presser foot to avoid hitting them with sewing machine needle. Or, remove them before they move under the presser foot. Due to the size and bulk of safety pins, they must be removed before stitching.

An alternative to pinning is basting. Basting stitches are large over/under running stitches worked through all layers. Since they are temporary, it is not necessary to knot the ends when starting and stopping. Use a contrasting color of thread to make the basting stitches easy to see and to remove.

Mitered Corners

Center a border strip along one side of quilt top; there will be overlap at each end. Sew to side, beginning and ending ¼" from each edge, **Fig 2**. Repeat for remaining three sides. To make a mitered or diagonal corner seam,

Fig 2

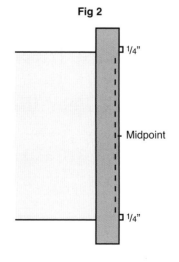

¼"

Midpoint

¼"

fold quilt in half diagonally allowing border strips to line up evenly, **Fig 3**.

Fig 3

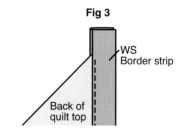

WS
Border strip

Back of quilt top

Draw diagonal line on border strip even with fold in quilt; sew on drawn line going from inside to outside corner, **Fig 4**. Check miter, then trim excess fabric ¼" from seam. Press seam open. Repeat at three remaining corners.

Fig 4

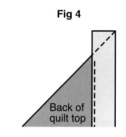

Back of quilt top

Marking the Quilting Pattern

Mark a uniform quilting pattern with an air-soluble marking pen or with quilters' chalk. For a quilting pattern that follows the piecing pattern or for a free-form pattern, there is no need to mark the quilt top before quilting.

Machine Quilting

When quilting by machine, work from the center out. Stitch at a slower speed and use a longer stitch length than for ordinary machine stitching. Reverse direction for two or three stitches at the beginning and end of each seam to prevent unraveling. Trim thread ends often while quilting. Use both hands while feeding the fabric under the presser foot.

Hand Quilting

Use 18" lengths of quilting or cotton thread. Knot one end and with one strand of thread, stitch small running stitches along seams and/or marked lines. Knot at the back and pull slightly to hide the knot under the quilt back.

Couching

Arrange the yarn on the quilt top. Use matching sewing thread and from the back to the front, insert the needle next to the yarn. Make a small tacking stitch to secure the yarn to the quilt top. Hold the yarn in place with your left hand, and continue stitching with your right hand to secure the entire length of yarn, **Fig 5**. Knot the thread at the back.

Fig 5

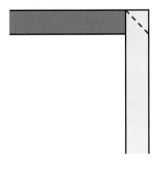

Binding

Trim edges of backing, batting and the quilt top to a straight and flush edge. Sew binding strips together diagonally to form one long strip, **Fig 6**; clip excess ¼" from seam. Fold binding in half lengthwise with wrong sides together.

Fig 6

Leave first few inches of binding unattached; then, matching raw edges, stitch binding to quilt top with a ¼" seam allowance, **Fig 7**. At corners, stop ¼" from edges; fold binding at a right angle, turn the quilt and continue stitching, **Fig 8**. When returning to the starting point, fold edge of lower binding under and overlap opposite end; finish sewing, **Fig 9**. Fold binding around to back of quilt, and hand stitch folded edge covering seam just sewn.

Fig 7

Fig 8

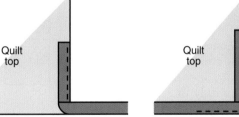

Fig 9

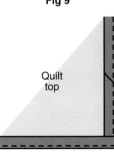

Facing

Trim edges of backing, batting and quilt top to a straight and flush edge. Cut strips 3" wide and the same length as the quilt. Place strips right sides together with quilt and stitch to sides of the quilt, **Fig 10**. Press strips away from seam line, fold to the back of the quilt and pin in place. Turn raw edge of facing under and hand-stitch to quilt back. Cut strips 3" longer than width of the quilt. Center, then stitch strips to top and bottom of quilt. Fold ends of the strips in so that they are flush with quilt sides facing under back, **Fig 11**. Press strips away from seam line, fold to back of quilt and pin in place. Turn raw edge of facing under and hand-stitch to quilt back.

Fig 10

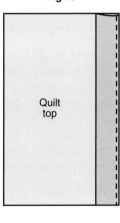

Quilt top

Fig 11

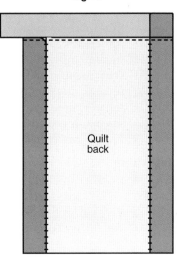

Quilt back

Autumn Leaves Quilt

Approximate Size: 27½" x 27½"

Materials

Fat quarter lt background (blocks)
12" square each, lt, med and dk gold, lt, med and dk red, lt, med and dk green (blocks)
¾ yd gold print (sashing)
½ yd burgundy (binding)
1 yd fabric (backing)
1 yd cotton batting
Air-soluble marking pen
Coordinating sewing thread for piecing and quilting
Contrasting sewing thread for machine embroidery
Quilter's chalk (optional)

Cutting Requirements

Gold Leaf Blocks

6 – 2½" squares, lt gold (A)
3 – 2⅞" squares cut in half diagonally, lt gold (B)
3 – 2½" squares, med gold (C)
3 – 2½" squares, dk gold (D)
3 – 2⅞" squares cut in half diagonally, dk gold (E)
3 – 2½" squares, lt background (F)
6 – 2⅞" squares cut in half diagonally lt background (G)

Red Leaf Blocks

2 – 3¼" squares cut in quarters diagonally, lt red (H)
6 – 2⅞" squares cut in half diagonally, med red (I)
6 – 2⅞" squares cut in half diagonally, dk red (J)
2 – 3¼" squares cut in quarters diagonally, dk red (K)
9 – 2½" squares, lt background (F)
3 – 3¼" squares cut in quarters diagonally, lt background (L)

Green Leaf Blocks

6 – 2½" squares, lt green (M)
2 – 2⅞" squares cut in half diagonally, lt green (N)
6 – 2½" squares, med green (O)
2 – 2⅞" squares cut in half diagonally, med green (P)
3 – 2½" squares, dk green (Q)
3 – 2⅞" squares cut in half diagonally, dk green (R)
3 – 2½" squares, lt background (F)
3 – 2⅞" squares cut in half diagonally, lt background (G)

Finishing

6 – 2½" x 6½" strips, gold print fabric (sashing)
2 – 2½" x 22½" strips, gold print fabric (sashing)
4 – 3½" x 29" strips (border)
3 – 5¼"-wide strips burgundy (binding)

Instructions

1. Make three Gold Leaf blocks, **Fig 1**, three Red Leaf blocks, **Fig 2**, and three Green Leaf blocks, **Fig 3**.

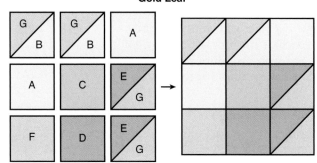

Fig 1
Gold Leaf

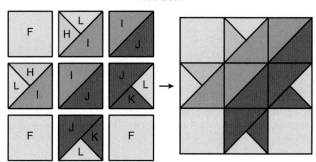

Fig 2
Red Leaf

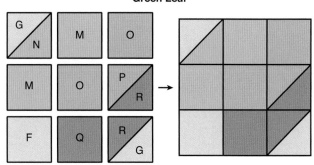

Fig 3
Green Leaf

2. Referring to **Layout**, place Leaf blocks in three rows of three blocks. Sew a 2½" x 6½" strip between the blocks to make three horizontal rows. Press seams to one side. Sew 2½" x 22½" strips between the horizontal rows; press.

3. Sew 3½" x 29" strips to sides of quilt referring to Mitered Corners, page 2, to complete corners.

4. With marking pen, and referring to **Figs 4**, **5** and **6**, mark placement of the veins/stems on all Leaf blocks.

5. Layer and baste quilt referring to Pinning & Basting, page 2.

6. Machine-quilt as desired referring to Machine Quilting, page 2. Remove pins or basting stitches. Trim the thread ends. Adjust sewing machine to desired line width and coverage for the machine-embroidered stems/veins. The width of those on the photographed quilt is ¹⁄₁₆". With the selected threads, stitch diagonal lines through all layers. Trim thread ends.

7. Trim edge of quilt. Referring to Binding, page 3, stitch binding around edge of quilt. ***Note:*** *This is a wide binding, therefore sew to quilt using a ⅞" seam allowance rather than the usual ¼" seam allowance.*

Fig 4
Gold Leaf

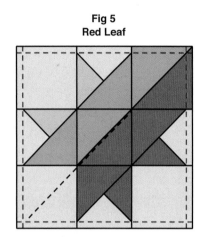

Fig 5
Red Leaf

Fig 6
Green Leaf

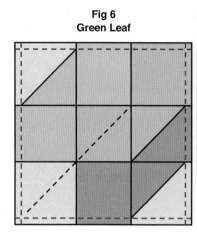

Autumn Leaves Quilt Layout

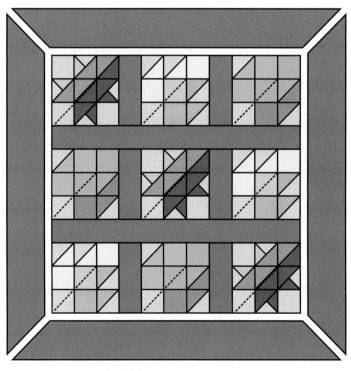

Springtime Quilt

Approximate Size: 36" x 42"

Materials

1½ yds white (blocks, plain squares)
12" squares blues, pinks, purples, red, green, brown (see photo and Cutting Requirements for colors used)
½ yd purple (binding)
1¼ yds backing fabric
1¼ yds cotton batting
Air-soluble marking pen
10 glass beads
Navy embroidery floss
Coordinating sewing thread for piecing and quilting
Contrasting sewing thread for machine embroidery
Quilter's chalk (optional)

Cutting Requirements

Cherry Blocks

15 – 2½" squares, white (A)
3 – 2⅞" squares cut in half diagonally, white (B)
24 – 1" squares, white (C)
6 – 2½" squares, red (D)
3 – 2⅞" squares cut in half diagonally, green (E)

Blossom Blocks

4 – 2⅞" squares cut in half diagonally, white (A)
2 – 3¼" squares cut in quarters diagonally, white (B)
2 – 2½" squares, yellow (C)
4 – 2⅞" squares cut in half diagonally, lt pink (D)
2 – 3¼" squares cut in quarters diagonally, med pink (E)
4 – 2⅞" squares cut in half diagonally, dk pink (F)

Nest Blocks

6 – 2⅞" squares cut in half diagonally, white (A)
3 – 2½" squares, rust (B)
6 – 2⅞" squares cut in half diagonally, rust (C)
3 – 2⅞" squares cut in half diagonally, brown (D)
12 – 1½" squares, brown (E)
3 – 1½" x 2½" rectangles, brown (F)
6 – 1½" squares, blue (G)
3 – 1½" x 2½" rectangles, tan (H)
3 – 2⅞" squares cut in half diagonally, tan (I)

Purple Butterfly Blocks

12 – 2½" squares, white (A)
2 – 3¼" squares cut in quarters diagonally, white (B)
6 – ¾" squares, white (C)
3 – 2½" squares, dk purple (D)
2 – 2⅞" squares cut in half diagonally, dk purple (E)
3 – 3¼" squares cut in quarters diagonally, dk pink (F)
2 – 2⅞" squares cut in half diagonally, lt purple (G)
3 – 2½" squares, lt purple (H)
2 – 3¼" squares cut in quarters diagonally, lt pink (I)

Bird Blocks

20 – 2½" squares, white (A)
5 – ¾" squares, white
8 – 2⅞" squares cut in half diagonally, white (B)
2 – 3¼" squares cut in quarters diagonally, white (C)
5 – 2½" squares, dk blue (D)
5 – 2⅞" squares cut in half diagonally, dk blue (E)
3 – 2⅞" squares cut in half diagonally, lt blue (F)
3 – 2⅞" squares cut in half diagonally, med blue
2 – 3¼" squares cut in quarters diagonally, med blue (G)

Turquoise Butterfly

24 – 2½" squares, white (A)
12 – 2⅞" squares cut in half diagonally, white (B)
12 – 2⅞" squares cut in half diagonally, dk turquoise (C)
6 – 2½" squares, lt turquoise (D)

Flower Bud Blocks

60 – 2½" squares, white (A)
12 – 2⅞" squares cut in half diagonally, white (B)
6 – 3¼" squares cut in quarters diagonally, white (C)
48 – 1" squares, white (D)
12 – 2½" squares, purple (E)
12 – 2½" squares, yellow (F)
6 – 3¼" squares cut in quarters diagonally, green (G)

Finishing

8 – 6½" squares, white (plain squares)
5 – 2½"-wide strips, purple (binding)

Instructions

1. Make 12 Flower Bud blocks, **Fig 1**, two Blossom blocks, **Fig 2**, three Cherries blocks, **Fig 3**, three Nest blocks, **Fig 4**, three Purple Butterfly blocks, **Fig 5**, six Turquoise Butterfly blocks, **Fig 6** and five Bird blocks, **Fig 7**.

Fig 1
Flower Bud

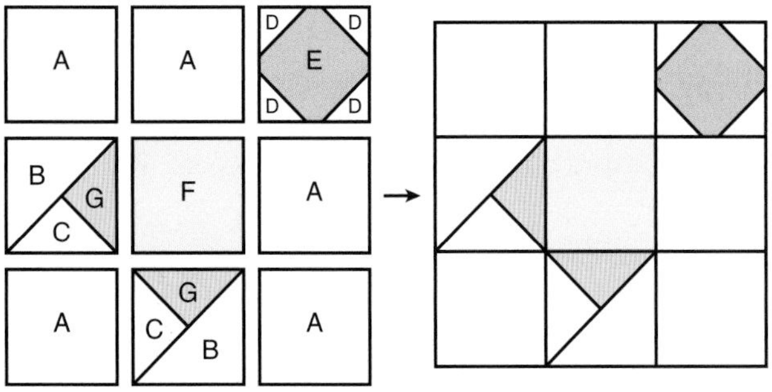

Fig 2
Blossom

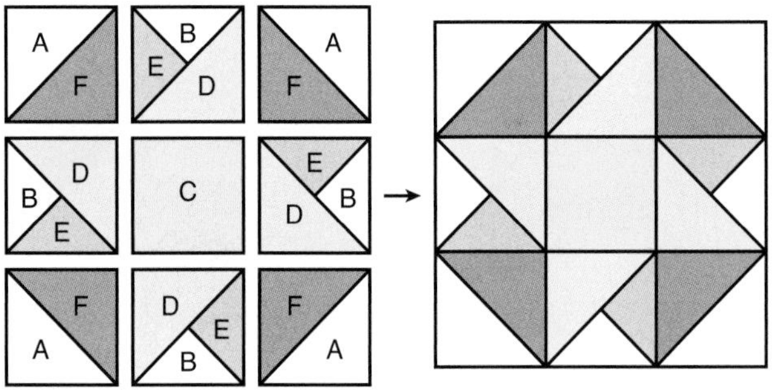

Fig 3
Cherries

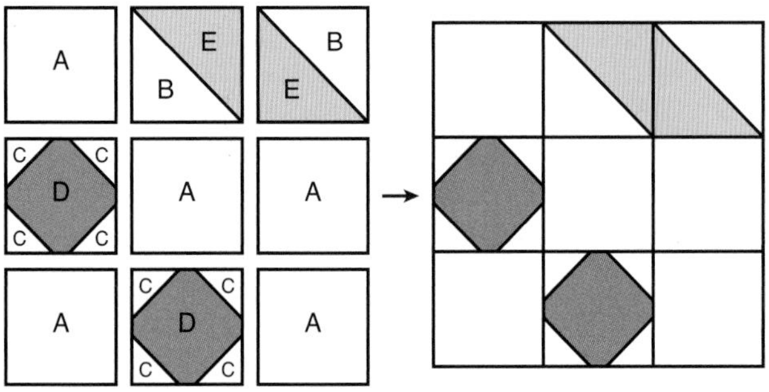

Fig 4
Nest

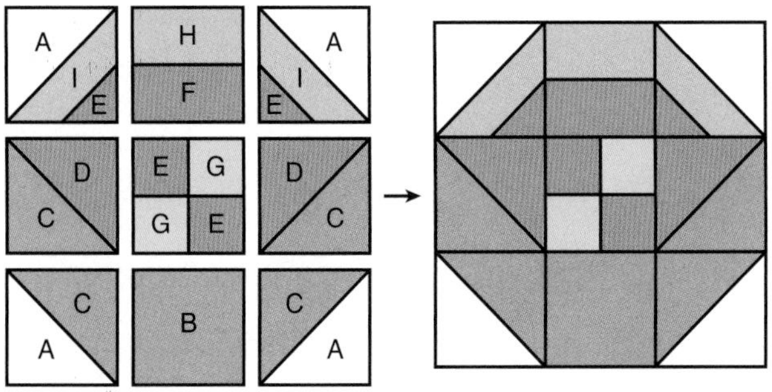

Fig 5
Purple Butterfly

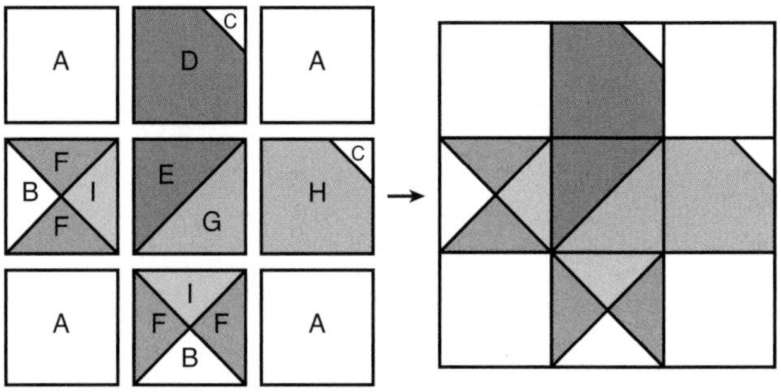

Fig 6
Turquoise Butterfly

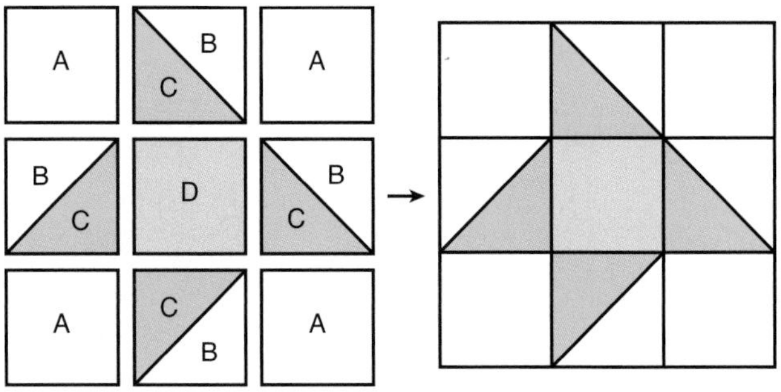

Fig 7
Bird

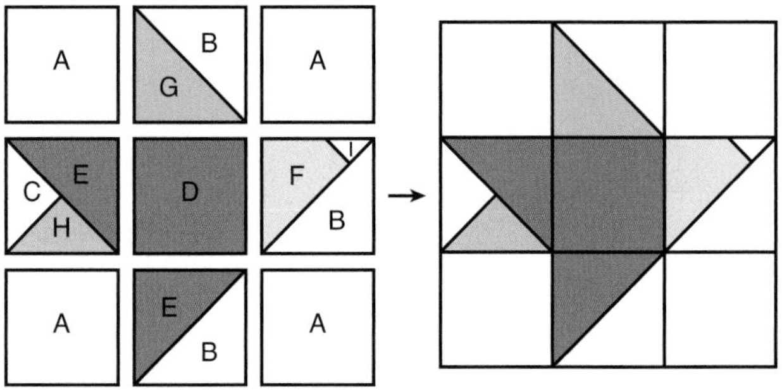

2. Referring to **Layout**, place white squares and pieced blocks in seven rows of six squares. Stitch squares and blocks together; press seams to one side, alternating directions in adjacent rows.

3. With marking pen, and referring to **Figs 8**, **9**, **10**, **11** and **12**, mark placement of the block details for machine embroidery: flower bud stems, cherry stems, butterfly bodies and antennae, blossom centers. Mark flower bud centers for bead placement and birds for eye placement.

Fig 8
Flower Bud

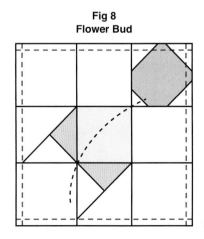

Fig 9
Blossom

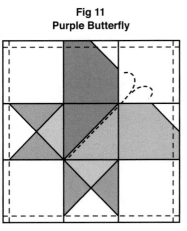

Fig 10
Cherries

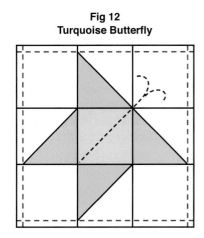

Fig 11
Purple Butterfly

Fig 12
Turquoise Butterfly

4. Use marking pen or quilter's chalk to mark quilting lines, if desired.

5. Layer and baste quilt referring to Pinning & Basting, page 2.

6. Machine-quilt as desired. (See Machine Quilting, page 2.) Remove pins or basting stitches. Trim thread ends. Adjust machine to desired line width and coverage for the machine-embroidered accents. The width of the stitching on the photographed model is ¹⁄₁₆". With the selected threads, stitch the marked lines through all layers. Trim thread ends. Trim edge of quilt.

7. Hand-stitch beads to flower centers. With embroidery floss, hand-stitch cross-stitches for birds' eyes.

8. Referring to Binding, page 3, stitch binding around edge of quilt.

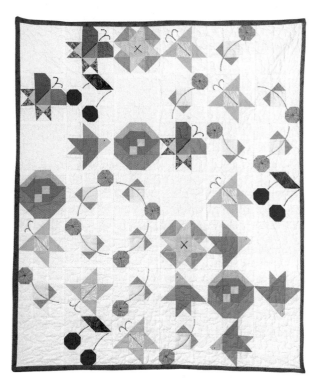

Springtime Quilt Layout

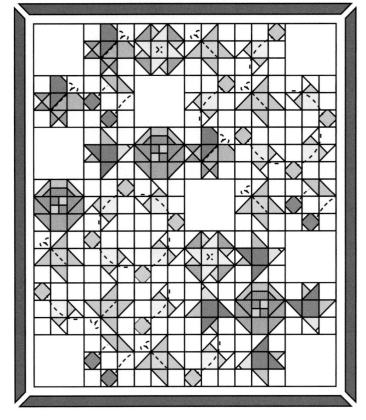

Sailboat Quilt

Approximate Size: 30" x 30"

Materials

⅛ yd red
⅓ yd yellow
¼ yd blue
¼ yd blue print
¼ yd white
⅜ yd med yellow (binding)
1 yd backing fabric
1 yd batting
Air-soluble marking pen
Coordinating sewing thread for piecing and quilting
Quilter's chalk

Cutting Requirements

Sailboat Blocks

15 – 2½" squares, blue (A)
10 – 2⅞" squares cut in half diagonally, blue (B)
5 – 2½" squares, white (C)
5 – 2⅞" squares cut in half diagonally, white (D)
5 – 2½" squares, red (E)
5 – 2⅞" squares cut in half diagonally, red (F)

Nine Patch Blocks

40 – 2½" squares, white
32 – 2½" squares, lt yellow

Finishing

4 – 4½" x 18½" strips, lt yellow (first border)
18 – 2⅞" squares cut in half diagonally, blue (second border)
18 – 2⅞" squares cut in half diagonally, white (second border)
4 – 2½"-wide strips, med yellow (binding)

Instructions

1. Make five Sailboat Blocks, **Fig 1**.

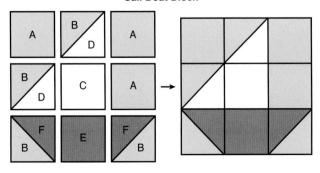

**Fig 1
Sail Boat Block**

2. Make eight basic Nine-Patch blocks, **Fig 2**.

Fig 2

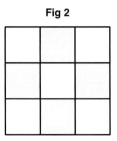

3. Place Sailboat and Nine-Patch blocks referring to **Layout**. Sew together in rows then sew rows together.

4. Sew white and blue border triangles together, **Fig 3**. Sew nine triangle squares together for border strip; note placement of triangle squares. Repeat for three more border strips.

Fig 3

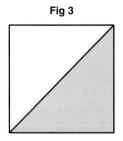

Sailboat Quilt Layout

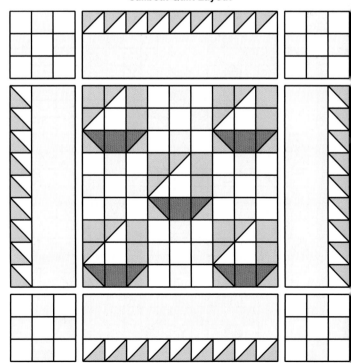

5. Sew blue/white pieced border strip to 4½"-wide yellow strip; repeat. Sew to sides of quilt.

6. Sew a Nine Patch block to each end of remaining border strips; sew to top and bottom of quilt.

7. Layer and baste referring to Pinning and Basting, page 3.

8. Machine-quilt as desired referring to Machine-Quilting, page 2.

9. Referring to Binding, page 3, attach binding.

Favorite Things Quilt

Approximate Size: 29" x 37¾"

Materials

12" squares tan, pink, turquoise, blue, purple, pink solid, lt pink print, dk pink print, dk green, med green dot, lt yellow, green
¼ yd white/blue print
¾ yd med yellow
⅜ yd peach print (binding)
1⅛ yds backing fabric
1⅛ yds batting
Air-soluble marking pen
Coordinating sewing thread for piecing and quilting
Green sewing thread for machine embroidery
Quilter's chalk

Cutting Requirements

Pinwheel Blocks

12 – 2½" squares tan (A)
6 – 2⅞" squares cut in half diagonally, tan (B)
2 – 2⅞" squares cut in half diagonally each, pink, turquoise, blue, purple (C, E, G, I)
1 – 3¼" square cut in quarters diagonally each, pink, turquoise, blue, purple (D, F, H, J)

Heart Blocks

6 – 2½" squares, blue (A)
8 – 2⅞" squares cut in half diagonally, blue (B)
1 – 3¼" square cut in quarters diagonally, blue (C)
2 – 2⅞" squares cut in half diagonally, pink solid (D)
3 – 3¼" squares cut in quarters diagonally, pink solid (E)
8 – 2⅞" squares cut in half diagonally, lt pink print (F)
2 – 3¼" squares cut in quarters diagonally, dk pink print (G)

Bow Tie Blocks

6 – 2½" squares tan (A)
6 – 2⅞" squares cut in half diagonally, tan (B)
3 – 2½" squares, dk green (C)
6 – 2½" squares, med green dot (D)
6 – 2⅞" squares cut in half diagonally, med green dot (E)

Thistle Blocks

6 – 2½" squares, lt yellow (A)
12 – 1½" squares, lt yellow (B)
15 – 1½" x 2½" rectangles, lt yellow (C)
2 – 2⅞" squares cut in half diagonally, lt yellow (D)
9 – 1½" squares, purple (E)
2 – 2⅞" squares cut in half diagonally, purple (F)
3 – 1½" squares, green (G)
9 – 1½" x 2½" rectangles, green (H)

Finishing

31 – 3¼" x 6½" strips, med yellow
4 – 2½"-wide strips, peach print
20 – 3¼" squares, white/blue print

Instructions

1. Make three Thistle blocks, **Fig 1**, three Heart blocks, **Fig 2**, three Bow Tie blocks, **Fig 3**, and three Pinwheel blocks, **Fig 4**.

Fig 1
Thistle

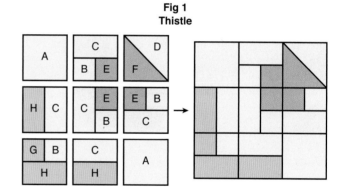

Fig 2
Heart

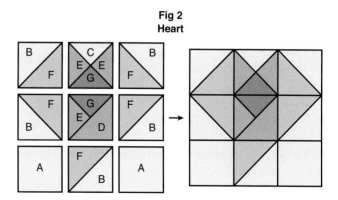

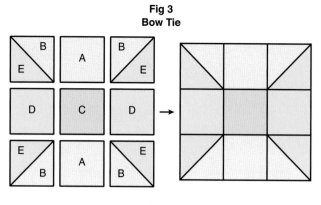

Fig 3
Bow Tie

Fig 4
Pinwheel

5. Refer to Pinning & Basting, page 2, to layer and baste your quilt. Machine-quilt as desired (see Machine Quilting, page 2).

6. Adjust your machine to desired line width and coverage for the machine-embroidered stems. The width of the stems on the photographed quilt is $\frac{1}{16}$". With the green thread, stitch diagonal lines through all layers.

7. Refer to Binding, page 3, to attach binding.

2. Place blocks referring to photo and **Layout**. Sew blocks together in rows alternating with the 3¼" x 6½" med yellow strips. Sew four white/blue print squares alternately with three 3¼" x 6½" med yellow strips; repeat four more times.

3. Sew strip rows and block rows together.

4. With marking pen and referring to **Fig 5**, mark the stems for machine embroidery.

Fig 5
Thistle

Favorite Things Quilt Layout

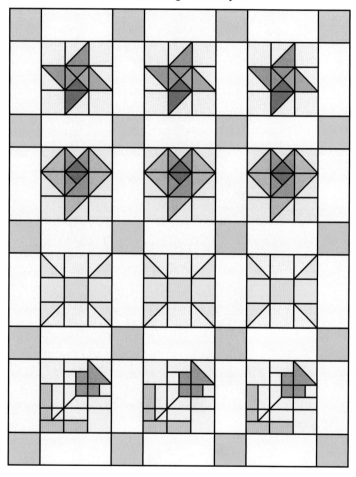

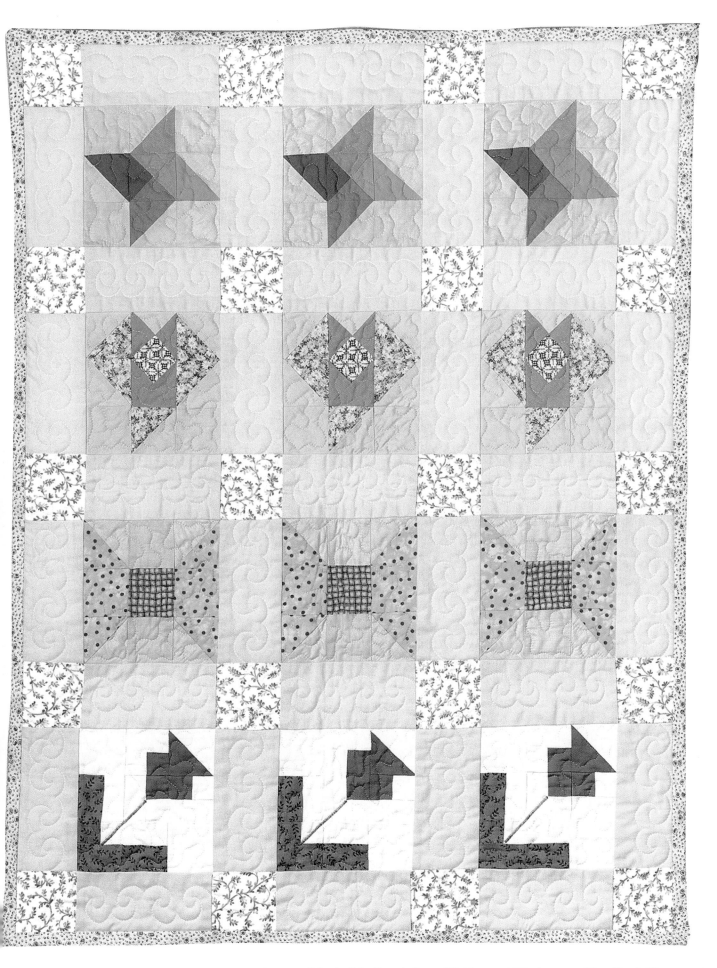

Three Bears Quilt

Approximate Size: 33" x 39"

Materials

12" squares of assorted fabrics (lt aqua, dk aqua, gold, white, lavender, brown, tan, gray, off-white, green, blue, lt red, black, dk red)
¼ yd med yellow fabric (first border)
1 yd dk yellow print (second border)
⅜ yd dk yellow print (binding)
1¼ yds backing fabric
1¼ yds batting
Air-soluble marking pen
Coordinating sewing thread for piecing and quilting
Contrasting sewing thread for machine embroidery
Quilter's chalk

Cutting Requirements

Goldilocks Block

3 – 2½" squares, lt aqua (A)
1 – 3¼" square cut into quarters diagonally, lt aqua (B)
1 – 2⅞" square cut in half diagonally, lt aqua (C)
1 – 3¼" square cut in quarters diagonally, dk aqua (D)
2 – 2⅞" squares cut in half diagonally, gold (E)
1 – 3¼" square cut in quarters diagonally, gold (F)
2 – 2⅞" squares cut in half diagonally, white (G)

Bowl Blocks

9 – 2½" squares, white (A)
6 – 2⅞" squares cut in half diagonally, white (B)
2 – 3¼" squares cut in quarters diagonally, white (C)
6 – 2½" squares, lavender (D)
3 – 2⅞" squares cut in half diagonally, lavender (E)
2 – 3¼" squares cut in quarters diagonally, lavender (F)

Bear Blocks

4 – 2½" squares each, brown, tan, gray (A)
2 – 2⅞" squares each, brown, tan, gray cut in half diagonally (B)
1 – 3¼" square each, brown, tan, gray cut in half diagonally (C)
1 – 1½" x 2½" rectangle each, brown, tan, gray (D)
3 – 2½" squares, off-white (E)
1 – 3¼" square cut in quarters diagonally, off-white (F)
3 – 2⅞" squares cut in half diagonally, lavender (G)
18 – 1" squares, lavender (H)
3 – 1½" x 2½" rectangles, lavender (I)

Pine Tree Blocks

4 – 2½" squares, green (A)
5 – 2⅞" squares cut in half diagonally, green (B)
4 – 2½" squares, blue (C)
5 – 2⅞" squares cut in half diagonally, blue (D)

House Block

2 – 2½" squares, lt red (A)
1 – 2⅞" square cut in half diagonally, lt red (B)
3 – 2⅞" squares cut in half diagonally, black (C)
2 – 1½" x 2½" rectangles, dk red (D)
2 – 2⅞" squares cut in half diagonally, blue (E)
2 – 1½" x 2½" rectangles, blue (F)

Nine-Patch Blocks

30 – 2½" squares, lavender
24 – 2½" squares, white

Finishing

2 – 2" x 18½" strips, med yellow (first border)
2 – 2" x 27½" strips, med yellow (first border)
2 – 6½" x 21½" strips, dk yellow print (second border)
2 – 6½" x 27½" strips, dk yellow print (second border)
4 – 2½"-wide strips dk yellow print (binding)

Instructions

1. Make one Goldilocks block, **Fig 1**, three Bowl blocks, **Fig 2**, three Bear blocks, **Fig 3**, two Pine Tree blocks, **Fig 4**, and one House block, **Fig 5**.

**Fig 1
Goldilocks**

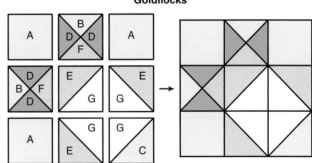

Fig 2
Bowl

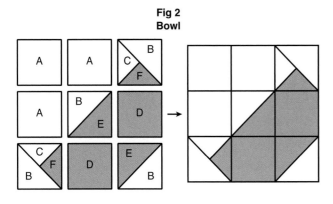

Fig 3
Bear

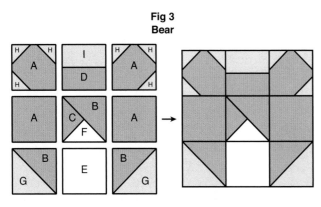

Fig 4
Pine Tree

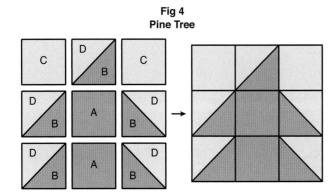

Fig 5
House

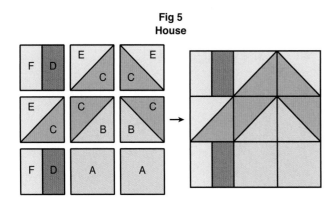

2. Make six white/lavender Nine Patch blocks, **Fig 6**.

Fig 6

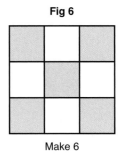

Make 6

3. Referring to photo and **Layout**, place blocks in rows. Sew blocks together in rows then sew rows together.

4. Sew med yellow border strips to top and bottom first, then to sides of quilt.

5. Sew dk yellow print border strips to top and bottom of quilt. Sew a Nine-Patch block to each end of remaining dk yellow print border strips, then sew to sides of quilt.

6. With marking pen and referring to **Fig 7**, **Fig 8**, **Fig 9** and **Fig 10**, mark embroidery accents on blocks.

7. Layer and baste quilt referring to Pinning & Basting, page 2.

Fig 7
Goldilocks

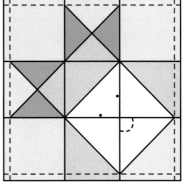

Fig 8
Bowl

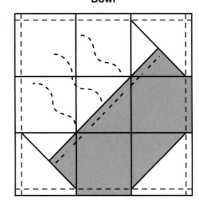

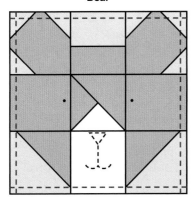

Fig 9
Bear

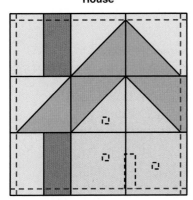

Fig 10
House

8. Machine-quilt as desired (see Machine Quilting, page 2).

9. Adjust sewing machine to desired line width and coverage for the machine-embroidered accents. The width of the stitching in the photographed model is ⅟₁₆". With selected threads, stitch on marked lines through all layers.

10. Refer to Binding, page 3, to attach binding.

Three Bears Quilt Layout

Going Places Quilt

Approximate Size: 34½" x 42"

Materials

Fat quarters lt lavender, lt red, dk red, white black, lt
    blue, lt yellow, med yellow, dk yellow, lt teal, dk teal,
    dk blue, pink
⅛ yd dk teal (sashing)
⅛ yd blue (sashing)
⅓ yd burgundy (inner border)
½ yd facing fabric
Assorted print and pastel fabrics at least 6½" wide for border
1¼ yds backing fabric
1¼ yds batting
Air-soluble marking pen
Coordinating sewing thread for piecing and quilting
Contrasting sewing thread from machine embroidery
Quilter's chalk

Cutting Requirements

Red Car Blocks
8 – 2½" lt lavender (A)
2 – 2⅞" squares cut in half diagonally, lt lavender (B)
36 – ¾" squares, lt lavender (C)
8 – 2½" squares, lt red (D)
4 – 2⅞" squares cut in half diagonally, lt red (E)
4 – 2½" squares, dk red (F)
2 – 2⅞" squares cut in half diagonally, white (G)
8 – 2½" squares, black (H)

Yellow Car Blocks
6 – 2½" lt blue (A)
2 – 2⅞" squares cut in half diagonally, lt blue (B)
27 – ¾" squares, lt blue (C)
6 – 2½" squares, lt yellow (D)
3 – 2⅞" squares cut in half diagonally, lt yellow (E)
3 – 2½" squares, dk yellow (F)
2 – 2⅞" squares cut in half diagonally, white (G)
6 – 2½" squares, black (H)

Teal Car Blocks
4 – 2½" squares, lt blue (A)
1 – 2⅞" square cut in half diagonally, lt blue (B)
18 – ¾" squares, blue (C)
4 – 2½" squares, lt teal (D)
2 – 2⅞" squares cut in half diagonally, lt teal (E)
2 – 2½" squares, dk teal (F)
1 – 2⅞" square cut in half diagonally, white (G)
4 – 2½" squares, black (H)

Rocket Blocks
4 – 2½" squares, dk blue (A)
5 – 2⅞" squares cut in half diagonally, dk blue (B)
4 – 2½" squares, pink (C)
5 – 2⅞" squares cut in half diagonally, lt red

Kite Block
5 – 2½" squares, lt blue (A)
2 – 1½" x 2½" rectangles, lt blue (B)
2 – 2½" squares, dk red (C)
2 – 1½" x 2½" rectangles, dk red (D)

Man Block
3 – 2½" squares, med yellow (A)
2 – 2⅞" squares cut in half diagonally, med yellow (B)
4 – ¾" squares, med yellow (C)
1 – 2½" square, white (D)
1 – 2½" square, dk red (E)
2 – 2⅞" squares cut in half diagonally, dk red

Finishing
3 – 1½" x 18½" strips, teal (sashing)
3 – 2" x 18½" strips, blue (sashing)
2 – 2½" x 18½" strips, burgundy (inner border)
2 – 2½" x 26" strips, burgundy (inner border)
4 – 2½" squares, lt blue (inner border corners)
4 – 6½" squares, assorted fabrics (outer border corners)
Assorted squares and rectangles at least 6½" wide (outer
    border)
2 – 4¼" x 42" strips, facing fabric
2 – 4¼" x 35½" strips, facing fabric

Instructions

1. Make nine Car blocks, **Fig 1** (four red, three yellow and
two teal), two Rocket blocks, **Fig 2**, one Kite block, **Fig 3**
and one Man block, **Fig 4**.

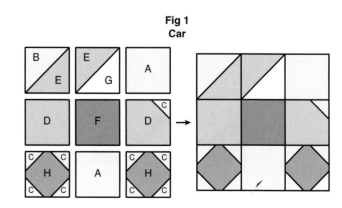

Fig 1
Car

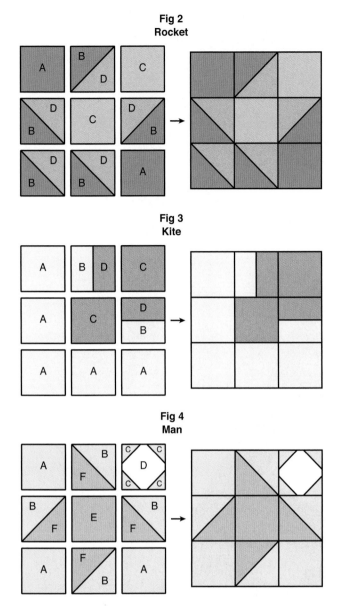

Fig 2
Rocket

Fig 3
Kite

Fig 4
Man

Note: When sewing a smaller square onto a large square such as sewing the C squares onto the H squares in the Car blocks, use the stitch and flip technique. Place the small square right sides together on one corner of the larger square. Sew diagonally from corner to corner of the small square. Trim corner ¼" from seam and fold back resulting small triangle.

2. Place Car blocks in rows referring to photo and **Layout**. Sew blocks together in rows.

3. Sew teal strips to bottom of each car row. Stitch blue strips to teal strips.

4. Sew burgundy strips to top and bottom of quilt. Sew a lt blue square to each end of remaining burgundy strips, then sew to sides of quilt top.

5. Referring to photo, sew Man block to Kite block, then sew to assorted 6½"-wide squares and rectangles; strip should measure 22½" long. Sew to bottom of quilt top. Sew a Rocket block to assorted 6½"-wide squares and rectangles; strip should measure 22½" long. Sew to top of quilt.

6. Again referring to photo, sew a Rocket block to assorted 6½" squares and rectangles; strip should measure 30" long. Sew a 6½" square to each end and attach to right edge of quilt. Sew assorted 6½"-wide squares and rectangles together to make a strip 30" long. Sew a 6½" square to each end and attach to left edge of quilt.

7. With marking pen and referring to **Figs 5**, **6**, and **7**, draw embroidery details – rocket exhaust, wheel centers, kite ribs and kite string.

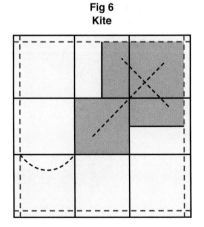

Fig 5
Car

Fig 6
Kite

**Fig 7
Rocket**

8. Layer and baste quilt referring to Pinning & Basting, page 2.

9. Adjust machine to desired line width and coverage for machine-embroidered accents. The width of the stitching on the photographed model is ⅟₁₆". With the selected threads, stitch on marked lines through all layers.

Going Places Quilt Layout

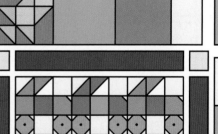

10. Sew a 4¼" x 42" facing strip to one side of quilt; press raw edge under ¼", then fold strip toward back of quilt until a nice edge is formed. Hand-stitch to back of quilt. Be careful not to let stitches show on front of quilt. Repeat on opposite side.

11. Sew 4¼" x 35½" facing strips to top and bottom of quilt; be sure there is a ½" overlap at each end. When folding strip toward back, tuck ends under to hide raw edges. Hand-stitch strips to backing.

Cats With Toys Quilt

Approximate Size: 31" x 31"

Materials

Fat quarters med gray, lt gray, dk gray, purple, white,
    lt blue, red
Scraps yellow, med blue
¾ yd white (sashing, first border)
¼ yd red print (second border)
¼ yd lt blue print
¼ yd blue rayon velvet
½ yd yellow print (binding)
1 yd backing fabric
1 yd batting
Air soluble marking pen
6 lavender beads
6 – ⅜" black sequins
Blue yarn
Blue thread to match yarn
Coordinating sewing thread for piecing and quilting
Contrasting sewing thread for machine embroidery
Quilter's chalk

Cutting Requirements

Cat blocks

3 – 2½" squares, med gray (A)
3 – 2⅞" squares cut in half diagonally, lt gray (B)
2 – 3¼" squares cut in quarters diagonally, lt gray (C)
5 – 3¼" squares cut in quarters diagonally, dk gray (D)
3 – 2⅞" squares cut in half diagonally, purple (E)
2 – 3¼" squares cut in quarters diagonally, purple (F)
6 – 2½" squares, white (G)
3 – 2⅞" squares cut in half diagonally, white (H)
2 – 3¼" squares cut in quarters diagonally, white (I)

Top Blocks

6 – 2½" squares, lt blue (A)
3 – 2⅞" squares cut in half diagonally, lt blue (B)
2 – 3¼" squares cut in quarters diagonally, lt blue (C)
3 – 1½" squares, lt blue (D)
3 – 1½" x 2½" rectangles, lt blue (E)
3 – 1½" squares, yellow (F)
3 – 2½" squares, purple (G)
2 – 2⅞" squares cut in half diagonally, purple (H)
2 – 3¼" squares cut in quarters diagonally, purple (I)
6 – 2½" squares, red (J)
2 – 2⅞" squares cut in half diagonally, med blue (K)

Finishing

3 – 6½" squares, lt blue print (yarn squares)
3 – 4"-wide circles, blue velvet (yarn)
6 – 2½" x 6½" strips, white (vertical sashing)
2 – 2½" x 22½" strips, white (horizontal sashing)
4 – 3½" x 28½" strips, white (first border)
4 – 1½" x 30½" strips, red print (second border)
4 – 3½"-wide strips, yellow print (binding)

Instructions

1. Make three Cat blocks, **Fig 1**, and three Top blocks, **Fig 2**.

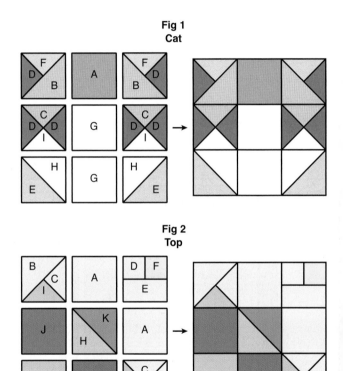

Fig 1
Cat

Fig 2
Top

2. With marking pen, referring to **Fig 3** and **Fig 4**, mark placement of the Cats' faces and Top details.

**Fig 3
Cat**

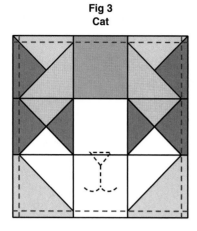

**Fig 4
Top**

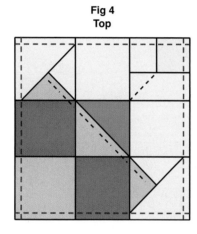

3. Center and pin velvet circles to 6½" lt blue squares. Cut four 12" lengths of yarn. Refer to **Fig 5** and place lengths parallel to each other on one circle. Cut six 8" lengths of yarn and place them on circle, overlapping the first four lengths at an angle. Cut four lengths of yarn and place them on circle, overlapping the second six lengths at an angle.

Fig 5

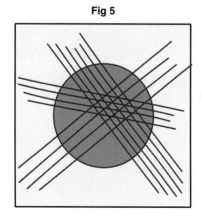

Adjust machine to a medium-width zigzag stitch. Using blue thread, zigzag around edge of circle, securing ends of yarn, **Fig 6**. Stitch a second row ¼" in from edge of circle. Trim all but one end of yarn flush with stitching. Repeat for remaining two circles.

Fig 6

4. Referring to photo and **Layout**, place blocks in rows. Sew 2½" x 6½" white strips between blocks to make three vertical rows. Press.

5. Sew 2½" x 22½" white strips between rows.

6. Referring to Mitered Corners, page 2, sew 3½" x 28½" white strips to quilt top.

7. Referring to Mitered Corners, sew 1½" x 30½" red print strips to quilt top.

8. Layer and baste referring to Pinning & Basting, page 2.

9. Adjust machine to desired line width and coverage for the machine-embroidered details. The width of those on the photographed model is ⅟₁₆". With selected threads, stitch marked lines through all layers. Hand stitch sequins and beads in place for the Cats' eyes.

10. Referring to photo for placement, draw X's at intersections between squares and around border. Each line measures 1¼". Using the blue yarn, stitch the X's. Knot at the back to secure.

11. Referring to Couching, page 3, make couching stitches to secure the parallel yarn strands and the single loose strands with blue thread, **Fig 7**.

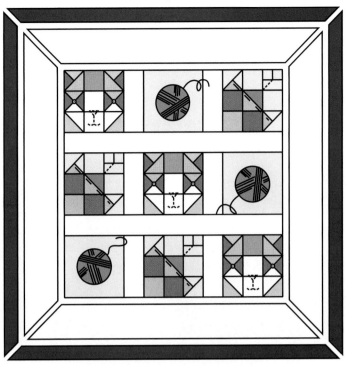

Fig 7

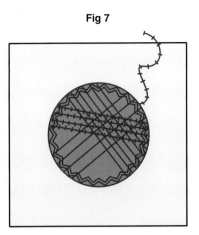

12. Refer to Binding, page 3, to attach binding. ***Note:*** *Sew binding to quilt with a ¾" seam allowance.*

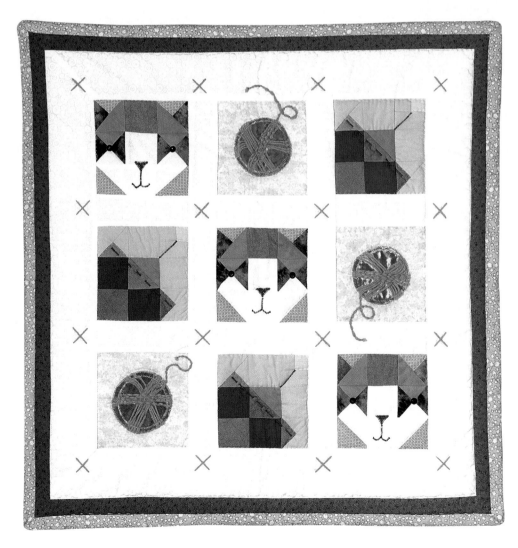

Corn & Pear Pillow

Pillow Size: 14" x 14"

Materials

Scraps lt yellow, dk yellow, lt gold, med gold, dk gold, green, white
¼ yd med gold print
¼ yd dk gold print
½ yd red fabric (includes backing)
14½" square batting
14" pillow form
Air-soluble marking pen
Coordinating sewing thread for piecing

Cutting Requirements

Corn Block

2 – 2½" squares, white (A)
3 – 2⅞" squares cut in half diagonally, white (B)
2 – 2½" squares, lt yellow (C)
1 – 2⅞" square cut in half diagonally, dk yellow (D)
2 – 2⅞" squares cut in half diagonally, green (E)

Pear Block

1 – 2½" square, white (A)
3 – 2⅞" squares cut in half diagonally, white (B)
1 – 3¼" square cut in quarters diagonally, white (C)
2 – 2½" squares, lt gold (D)
1 – 2⅞" square cut in half diagonally, lt gold (E)
2 – 2⅞" squares cut in half diagonally, med gold (F)
1 – 3¼" square cut in quarters diagonally, med gold (G)
1 – 2⅞" square cut in half diagonally, green (H)

Finishing

1 – 6½" square, med gold print
1 – 6½" square, dk gold print
1 – 14½" square, red (backing)
4 – 1½" x 14½" strips, red

Instructions

1. Make one Pear block, **Fig 1,** and one Corn block, **Fig 2.**

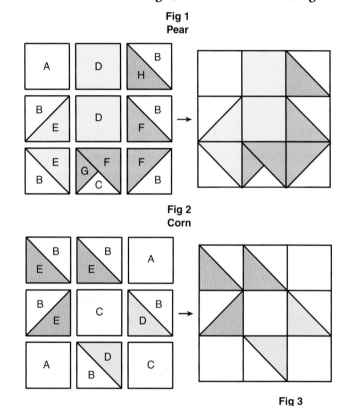

Fig 1
Pear

Fig 2
Corn

2. Sew Corn block to left side of med gold print square; sew Pear block to right side of dk gold print square. Sew the pairs together, **Fig 3.**

3. Referring to Mitered Corners, page 2, sew red strips to pillow center, **Fig 4.**

4. Center and place pillow top right sides together with pillow back; place batting on pillow top. Stitch through all layers leaving a 10" opening along bottom edge. Trim excess batting and fabric at corners. Turn right side out.

5. Insert pillow form and slipstitch opening closed.

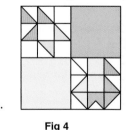

Fig 3

Fig 4

Peas & Tomato Pillow

Pillow Size: 14" x 14"

Materials

12" squares each, lt green, med green, dk green, med red
    print, dk red print, dk red, lt yellow, white
½ yd gold print
14½" square cotton batting
14" pillow form
Air-soluble marking pen
Coordinating sewing thread for piecing

Cutting Requirements

Tomato Block

3 – 2½" squares, dk red print (A)
2 – 2⅞" squares cut in half diagonally, med red print (B)
2 – 1½" squares, med red print (C)
2 – 1½" x 2½" rectangles, med red print (D)
1 – 2⅞" square cut in half diagonally, med green (E)
2 – 1½" squares, med green (F)
2 – 2⅞" squares cut in half diagonally, white (G)

Peas Block

1 – 2½" square, lt green (A)
3 – 2⅞" squares cut in half diagonally, lt green (B)
1 – 2⅞" square cut in half diagonally, dk green (C)
2 – 2½" squares, lt yellow (D)
2 – 2⅞" squares cut in half diagonally, lt yellow (E)

Finishing

1 – 6½" square, med red
1 – 6½" square, dk red
4 – 1½" x 14½" strips, gold (border)
1 – 14½" square, gold (backing)

Instructions

1. Make one Tomato block, **Fig 1**, and one Peas block, **Fig 2**.

Fig 1
Tomato

Fig 2
Peas

2. Sew Peas block to left side of med red print square; sew Tomato block to right side of dk red square. Sew the pairs together, **Fig 3**.

3. Referring to Mitered Corners, page 2, sew gold strips to pillow center, **Fig 4**.

4. Center and place pillow top right sides together with pillow back; place batting on pillow top. Stitch through all layers leaving a 10" opening along bottom edge. Trim excess batting and fabric at corners. Turn right side out.

5. Insert pillow form and slipstitch opening closed.

Fig 3

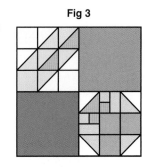

Fig 4

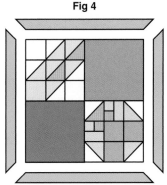

American School of Needlework®
excellence in instruction

DRG Publishing
306 East Parr Road
Berne, IN 46711
©2004 American School of Needlework
TOLL-FREE ORDER LINE or to request a free catalog (800) 582-6643
Customer Service (800) 282-6643, Fax (800) 882-6643

Visit AnniesAttic.com.

Customer Service (800) 282-6643, **fax** (800) 882-6643

ISBN:1-59012-102-3   All rights reserved.   Printed in USA   3 4 5 6 7 8 9